Praise for *Wh...*

I wish everyone could read this book so they will be prepared to support loved ones when a tragedy strikes. Excellent resource with practical steps to help a grieving friend.

> — *Mindy Daffron*
> *Trauma Intervention Program*
> *Crisis Team Manager*

You will enter this book awkward and unsure — you will emerge a confident, loving, and creative advocate for your grieving friend.

> — *Dr. Vicki K. Harvey*
> *Psychologist*

It is truly well done! It often takes a pastor a decade to gain the wisdom she has expressed.

> — *Dr. Clair MacMillan*
> *National Director at the Church of the Nazarene, Canada*

I am a psychologist who has not only experienced grief but have worked with others who are grieving. This book is an excellent resource. It is a quick and easy read with fabulous do's and don'ts. I think everyone should read it as it will be relevant for all of us at some point in our lives.

> — *M. Robinson*
> *Psychologist*

No one knows exactly how to respond to grief. Your friends look away and you can actually feel the tension in the room because there truly is no sure way to comfort someone who has just dealt with a loss of this magnitude. The author took it upon herself to let others know what she learned about grief and offers a "door" to those who are hurt and those who are trying desperately to find the right way to comfort them during this time. It is a fact that everyone grieves differently, but this author should be commended for tapping into her own traumatic experience to bring others a bit of peace.

— *Feathered Quill Book Reviews*

THIS BOOK HAS RECEIVED SEVERAL AWARDS

When Their World Stops

SECOND EDITION

The Essential Guide to TRULY Helping Anyone in Grief

When Their World Stops

SECOND EDITION

The Essential Guide to TRULY Helping Anyone in Grief

ANNE-MARIE LOCKMYER

Joseph Allen Press
Anaheim, California

WHEN THEIR WORLD STOPS:
The Essential Guide to TRULY Helping Anyone in Grief

Joseph Allen Press, Anaheim, CA

www.GriefandTraumaHealing.com

Book design by TLC Graphics, *www.TLCGraphics.com*
Cover: Monica Thomas, Interior: Erin Stark

Cover photo: istockphoto.com © PeopleImages

ISBN: 978-0-9968024-2-0

Printed in the United States of America.

Library of Congress Control Number: 2018901863

To contact the author or order additional copies of this book, email:
help@griefandtraumahealing.com

I am delighted to be able to present the second edition of *When Their World Stops.*

New experiences and interviews have allowed me to add updates. I continually hear inspirational stories from readers that need to be shared.

Included is an introduction to grief recovery, as I have experienced the transforming process of healing from my loss. When I wrote the first edition, I was in the midst of intense grief. Pain is real my friends! But so is HOPE!

Anne-Marie

An Important Note from the Author

PEOPLE GRIEVE DIFFERENTLY

WHAT I'M SHARING WITH YOU HERE ARE FEELINGS AND NEEDS that are very common in grief. However, each person's grief experience and journey are unique. So it's possible that a given person will not respond the way you might think. If this happens, rest assured that you have enough in this guide to help in some way. Just let the grieving person's responses guide you.

— Anne-Marie Lockmyer

P.S. I use the terms *they/them/their* throughout this book to easily cover both genders, knowing full well that, from a technical standpoint, this is grammatically incorrect. We all end up using *they/them/their* when we talk about people in the singular context, though. So to keep things both simple and conversational, I do the same thing here.

Our most difficult task
as a friend is to offer
understanding when
we don't understand.

ROBERT BRAULT

Dedication and Acknowledgments

THIS BOOK IS DEDICATED TO THE PRECIOUS FRIENDS WHO walked beside me through the most painful and difficult journey I have ever experienced — the people who cared for me when I had lost the love of my life, who cried with me and held me when I wanted to die, who did for me what I was incapable of doing for myself, who checked on me when everyone else left, who reached out on days they knew would be especially difficult for me. You taught me how to help the grieving.

A special thank you to those who shared their personal stories of grief with me so others could be helped.

To my son, Joseph, who has been my example of courage and endurance in the midst of constant suffering: You are my hero! "I'll love you forever and like you for always!"

In memory of my best friend and husband of twenty-six years, Mark Lockmyer — who loved and served others like no one I have ever met.

Table of Contents

The Back Story

IT'S 4:30 IN THE MORNING AS THE SHUTTLE VAN STOPS IN FRONT of my house to drive me to LAX. I'm heading off for a fun work trip to the Caribbean for a week.

My husband Mark and I kiss, have a big hug, and tell each other "I love you."

That memory is now forever ingrained in my mind: Standing in the driveway in the dark with my best friend, the love of my life.

For this would be our last kiss.

I've spent just one day at Club Med, and I'm having a great time with my coworkers. As I dress for dinner in my hotel room, the phone rings. My roommate answers and says, "It's for you."

I grab the phone and say, "Hello?"

"Anne-Marie, this is Julia," I hear on the other end. My heart sinks immediately. Julia is my husband's cousin, and if she's calling, it's something bad.

She tells me to sit down, which of course I don't.

"Just tell me, Julia! Tell me what's happened!"

"Anne-Marie, Mark died!"

"No! No! No! This can't be real!" I think to myself. "This can't be real! No!"

It was four days before our twenty-sixth wedding anniversary. Mark had suffered a brain aneurysm and had died in our bedroom. Our adult son had found him.

The world as I knew it stopped at that moment. It would NEVER be the same! I would NEVER be the same! The depth of the pain is unimaginable. The sounds that came out of me as I cried were like nothing I'd ever heard before.

Half of me was gone.

As I traveled the journey of grief over the next year, I saw how uncomfortable and awkward people were with me. They didn't know what to do. Some avoided me. It's true that, after the memorial service, pretty much everyone leaves; they move on. But I didn't.

I thus became very aware of the thoughtful and kind things people did. I also became aware of the thoughtless and hurtful things people did — without realizing it, of course. As a matter of fact, I had to apologize to friends of mine who had lost loved ones in the past, as I figured out that I had been one of the thoughtless ones in their lives during their time of pain. **Until you've experienced something like this, you just don't know.**

I kept noticing that most people have no clue how to talk to or support someone who is grieving. So someone, I thought, should write a book to guide people so that the grief of a person they care about no longer has to be awkward or something to be feared.

"Someone" turned out to be me.

Before Mark died, I would have needed a book like this one. My purpose in writing it is to encourage you and equip you to support the grieving person in your life. I want to help you understand what they are experiencing so that you can meet their needs — without having to guess about it all. Because I know firsthand that it's too easy to guess incorrectly.

If reading this book helps you comfort your grieving friend in any way you would not have been able to before, then I will consider it a success.

I had always considered myself a great friend — encouraging, there to help when needed, sensitive, able to see when people were suffering and how I might comfort them. But when my husband died so suddenly, I soon came to realize that, when it came to helping someone who was grieving … I KNEW VERY, VERY LITTLE!

As I began my own journey of grief, I became painfully aware that in the past I had not met the needs of my grieving friends as well as I'd believed. I thought I had known what to say and do, but I didn't. I thought I had understood how long their grieving should go on, but I didn't. I thought I had known what they should do, but I didn't.

Then there were the things I knew I hadn't known: what to say, what to ask. Should I talk about the grieving person's loved one or not? Should I mention the good things going on in my life? Should I mention a relationship I have that the grieving person has lost? Is it okay to watch a movie with them that could remind them of their loss? Should I invite them to a celebratory event like a birthday party or a wedding, as it could also remind them of their loss? Should I just avoid them so that I don't say anything wrong?

Talk about walking on eggshells.

When I joined a grief group, the first thing I learned was not to expect much from my friends so that I wouldn't be disappointed. And it was true. It's not that friends don't care or don't want to help. They just have no idea what to do or say. I was one of those friends myself. We are able to support our friends through many hard times, but when it comes to the death of a loved one it's like we get tongue-tied and paralyzed. We are fearful, desperately wanting to help but feeling inadequate to do so. Grief makes us uncomfortable, and we are at a loss as to what to do. Often we blurt out something we shouldn't. Or, sometimes, we simply do nothing.

I hope that what I've learned through my grief experience will help you be the friend you want to be to the grieving person in your life — the one you're trying to help right now. When we're not there for those who are grieving, it's not because we don't care; we do. **We just aren't sure how to respond. And we're scared.**

But we can do it. YOU can do it! And with a little knowledge and willingness, you will. Because you already have the most important quality you need to be helpful …

You care.

Maybe I can't stop
the downpour, but I will
always join you for
a walk in the rain.

So How Can You Help
— *Really* Help?

I'M PROBABLY GOING TO SHARE WITH YOU MORE INFORMATION than you want or need. That's by design; I would rather give you too much information than too little. But I want to make things as quick and easy as possible for you. **So if you want to skim this material to get the main points, read the bold print and the lists**. For more detail, read the rest. My own experiences are in *italics*.

My perspective is that of someone who has lost a spouse, but much of my experience would be the same for any type of loss, and I have included information from different perspectives throughout the book. **Specific types of losses** are addressed in more detail in the **Appendix**, which also offers more general tips if you would like them.

THE FIRST HOURS AND DAYS AFTER THE LOSS

Remember: Their World Has Stopped

For your grieving friend, the world has stopped. This loss is huge. They are probably in shock. So right now, just come alongside and be with them. Be sad with them. This is incredibly difficult for most of us, as we want to "fix it" and we can't. How can you fix a broken heart? Don't try. **The hardest thing to do is to simply be quiet and just be there. But don't try to "fix it" or make your grieving friend feel better. You can't!**

Let Them Grieve Their Own Way

Whatever your friend is doing as they are dealing with their grief is NORMAL. It's critical to understand: There is no "right way" to grieve. The grieving person may even do or say strange things; that's normal. *I found myself joking about my husband's death at times. I'm sure some people thought my comments were inappropriate, but it was my way of dealing with what had been handed to me.*

What Not to Say Matters

DO NOT say that the loss was for the best because your grieving friend's loved one was suffering ... or that God has a purpose in the loss ... or that God needed the loved one in Heaven ... or that it's fortunate the loss was quick ... or that at least your grieving friend had warning of the death to come ... or that the person who died lived a full life and will never hurt again ... or that time heals all wounds ... or that had the deceased person lived they would never have been the same ... or that it's "time to get on with your life" ... or that "you will have another child" or "you will get married again." These **platitudes don't make your friend feel better.**

And please: **Don't tell your grieving friend that you can relate** (even if you can). This type of statement puts the focus on you instead of them. One of my friends, who had lost her brother in a tragic accident, was told: "At least you didn't have to watch him die like I did when my dad died from cancer. Your situation was like a Band-Aid being taken off quickly to cause less pain. I watched my dad die a little every day for months. At least you went through it quickly." Not a clue.

Don't Tell Them They're Strong

Your grieving friend is probably numb and in shock. **They are not strong!**

Don't Tell Them How to Feel or What to Do

"You must be so relieved that he isn't suffering anymore." "You need to start moving on and dating." *If I had a dollar for every time someone talked to me about dating or how I needed to move on ...*

Be Honest and Sincere in What You *Do* Say

Things *to* say: "I am so, so sorry." "I don't know what to say, but I want you to know how much I care." "What are you feeling?" Acknowledge your grieving friend's pain. "This must be very difficult for you." "I've been thinking of you." "Why don't we go for a walk?" "We are all missing Mark. He was an incredible man and a good friend." "I cannot imagine your pain. I am here, and I love you!" Don't be afraid to say nothing, either, and simply hug your friend — assuming they like hugs. If they don't, you can simply grab their hand. Do what makes your grieving friend comfortable.

Use Touch

When you're grieving, it's comforting to have someone just sit there and hold your hand, hug you, run their hands over your head, or squeeze your shoulder. Nothing needs to be said. I loved when someone would let me hold their baby. It felt so good to be holding a person closely.

Bring Something

Would you like to bring something to your grieving friend? Meals are great. Breakfast foods can be a nice surprise. *One day someone brought me some bagels and cream cheese with small yogurts. It was especially thoughtful, as all the other meals that had been delivered were dinners, so we hadn't had anything for breakfast.*

You don't have to bring meals. Maybe you could bring bottles of water, drinks, paper plates and paper products, napkins, utensils, or tissues.

Don't plan to stay long when you drop things off. Sometimes it's best to come in, give your friend a hug and a card, drop off the food, and be on your way, unless it seems like they want you to stay.

Help Where You Can, *When* You Can

If your grieving friend lives out of town or is leaving town to take care of the details of an out-of-town loss, you may feel like you must do something NOW to help. But you can't do anything if your grieving friend isn't around — unless there are things that need to be done while they're gone, like taking care of a pet or watering the lawn or putting the garbage out.

Your friend is getting a lot of attention where they are. When they will REALLY need you is when they return. No one will care anymore, and people will expect your friend to return to normal life. That's when you will show up and be invaluable, as these are the darkest days.

Don't Ask — Just Do

Do not ask your grieving friend what they need, or to call you if they need anything. THEY HAVE NO IDEA WHAT THEY NEED! If there's something you want to do for them, just do it. Make the decision for them. Take it out of their hands.

If you think they could use some help getting their house ready for out-of-town guests, tell them you're coming over to clean it. Don't ask them if they need it cleaned. Don't ask them if they need food or meals, either. Tell them you're bringing food over. You can try asking what meal would be special to them or if there is something they are craving. If they can't answer, just bring them whatever you'd like.

Bottom line: SAY less and ASK less. DO more!

WHAT CAN YOU DO, EXACTLY?

For Starters, Be Dependable

Don't tell your grieving friend that you'll do something and then fail to follow through. This hurts more than not offering anything at all.

Think *very carefully* before you say anything casually in an effort to be a comfort or because it seems like the right thing to say. The danger — and the potential harm to your grieving friend — lies in you ultimately not doing what you said you would, especially when it comes to promises about the future:

- "We'll be there when everyone leaves."
- "I will come and fix things when you need it."
- "We will stand in for Joseph's father at special times, like birthdays and graduation."

These were promises made to me that were never kept. It really hurt. I know the people who said these things really didn't think about what they said — before or after. But when you're already broken-hearted from grief, broken promises only add to the pain.

Better to say nothing and then show up and do something. What a nice surprise!

I must acknowledge an angel named Jeff who called me almost monthly to see what needed to be done in my house and would come for a day to work on my list. He'd fix the garbage disposal and broken faucets, replace closet doors, install flooring, and much more. He took such a burden off of me. I would jump for joy every time he fixed something. His wife, Mary, played a part in it all as well: She was the one who would remind him to call, and she set up the schedule for him. What a pair!

I also had a technology angel named Woody who would make sure everything was working and would fix it when it didn't. Technology is another language for me. I had no idea how to fix the Internet when it was down, hook up printers, or repair computers. Woody's help was invaluable. He never acted like it was an imposition, but it was. When my laptop started to die, Woody and two other co-workers of Mark's bought me a beautiful new one and set it up for me. There are no words to express how touched and grateful I was for their incredible act of generosity in providing for such a practical need.

Set Up a Schedule

Set up a schedule for meals and tasks that need to get done so that everything is covered and you know who's doing what. There are some great programs to make this easy for you. One I liked was *carecalendar.org*. It is a free website to organize meals, errands, caring for the children, giving rides, housekeeping, etc. for families in need during a time of illness or life changing event.

Keep Track of Who *Did* What

Develop a list to keep track of who has helped with what. *It was all such a blur at times when I was so deep in my grief, and I wanted to thank the people who had helped me once things had slowed down a bit and I was doing better.*

Manage the Phone

Screen your grieving friend's phone calls for them so that they have time for critical basics like sleeping and eating. Many of the calls won't matter to them, but it is important to keep your friend rested and well nourished.

Manage Out-of-Town Guests

There may be out-of-town guests coming for the funeral service. Offer to help if they need a place to stay by finding them a hotel or providing a room in your house. If they're flying in, offer to pick them up from the airport. *This was a huge help to me and my guests. I felt bad that friends were offering to drive the long distance to and from the airport, but they would not let me protest. They insisted. One couple went to the airport four times and even took my guests out to lunch on the way to my place.*

On a related note: Find out how many people will be at the house on the day of the service and bring them all a good breakfast.

Manage Stressful People

Protect your grieving friend from difficult family members, friends, and situations. Your friend is already feeling so sad and overwhelmed. They don't need more stress. So tell the people who come around to behave. And if they don't, keep them away.

Help Keep Kids' Schedules as Normal as Possible

If your grieving friend has children, do whatever you can to help keep the kids' schedules normal (to the degree possible in such trying circumstances). Drive the children to and from activities. Take them out for ice cream or to friends' houses. Remember: Kids thrive on routine. Do what you can to help maintain it for them.

Do Housework

In the midst of the chaos of grief, it's nice to NOT have chaos in the house. Your grieving friend wants it to be as pleasant as possible to come home, and they don't want to be concerned about household chores on top of everything else they're dealing with.

So offer to take on some of this work. There's lots you can do:

- Take care of the laundry.
- Vacuum and wash the floors.
- Dust the place from top to bottom.
- Put dishes away. Or wash them (by hand or in the dishwasher).
- Wash sheets and remake fresh beds.
- Clean the bathrooms and make sure they are well stocked with toilet paper and soap.
- Sort things or paper.
- Go through the mail.
- Ask for a list of things your grieving friend needs or errands they need done. Drive your friend to the store, or watch their children so they can drive there themselves.
- Make meals.
- Make a grocery list and go shopping.
- Take care of the yard.
- Empty the garbage and put the garbage cans out.
- Wash the cars.
- Help your friend get their finances updated and in order.
- Walk the dogs.

- Clean up the cat's litter or the dog's poop in the yard.
- OR you can hire a cleaning service to come in for a day while you take your friend to lunch!

Have the Funeral/Memorial Service Videotaped

Arrange to have the memorial service or funeral videotaped so that your grieving friend can see it again later. *I loved watching the video of my husband's memorial service, because I was on autopilot the day it happened. I didn't even remember a lot of it. So it was very nice to be able to experience it again.*

Create a Photo Album

What a great opportunity to show your grieving friend how much you care, especially if you yourself knew the person who died for a long time.

Gather pictures of the person from others, and from your grieving friend. You undoubtedly have your own pictures too — ones your grieving friend has never seen.

The finished album doesn't have to be big, and you can either make it yourself or have it printed. Either way, your grieving friend will cherish it forever.

*One of my own friends **copied all of the Facebook posts of memories and well wishes** after my husband died and put them in a book. It took a long time to do, and I am so grateful. Now these treasures are saved forever!*

Help Deal with People and Paper

Your grieving friend needs someone to come and help them do the things that are needed right away: notifying family, friends, employers, Social Security; filling out forms of all kinds; figuring out life insurance, finances, bills; making memorial or funeral arrangements. Just having someone to **keep notes** and organize what needs to be done is invaluable. And notes need to be kept on everything that **has** been done, too. So **use a notebook**. Your grieving friend is truly in a daze much of the time and is not capable of remembering a lot of what's happening.

Some things need to be cancelled — memberships and the like. *My friend started a notebook for me with pockets where I could keep important papers as I was dealing with them. Everything that was done or that we were working on was kept in that notebook so that we always knew where to find things. It brought order to a situation that seemed so out of control.* The Legacy Binder, available on my website, includes a section on what to do after a death, as well as everything that should be done before a death occurs. It decreases the stress and makes things much easier at a time when it can be chaotic.

Be sure that your grieving friend gets lots of death certificates — between 10 and 25. They will need these certificates for so much of the paperwork and related tasks to come, not only in the short term but in the future as well.

Read Cards with Your Grieving Friend, and Encourage Your Friend to Keep Them in a Special Box

Your grieving friend will receive many cards and notes, and they will probably read the cards quickly and not remember them. So create a special box or chest, and present it to your friend so they can keep the cards and notes in it.

When things have slowed down a bit, open the box with your friend and read the cards and notes to them (or have your friend read the cards and notes aloud).

I have enjoyed reading the cards I received over and over again, especially when they feature stories about my husband that I hadn't heard before.

Manage the Thank-You Process

After the funeral or memorial service, and again when things slow down, bring thank-you notes, envelopes, and stamps to help your grieving friend express their gratitude.

Early on, make sure your friend has a place to keep track of who they'd like to eventually thank (or keep track of it all for them) — those bringing meals, helping out at the house, working on the funeral/memorial service, sending donations or flowers, and the like. It's very difficult for someone who's grieving to remember who brought or did what, and your friend will feel bad if they miss someone.

Schedule Companionship

Especially for the first week or two after the death, schedule people to be with your grieving friend daily to provide both company and assistance.

My friend made a list every day for the people who were coming to be with me so that they would know what to do. My friend scheduled the people to come and even told them when I needed a rest. It made things so much easier for the people who were helping; they knew what to do and didn't have to guess or wait for me to tell them. It relieved me so much!

CONVERSATIONS

Should You Talk About Your Grieving Friend's Loved One? Just Ask

Your grieving friend probably wants to talk about their loved one, and they probably want you to do the same. So instead of walking on eggshells, just come right out and ask. Once you know that your friend is OK with the idea, mention the lost loved one in conversation. It's okay to acknowledge the person who is gone. People sometimes believe that if they don't say anything about the person who died, their grieving friend won't remember the person is dead or will hurt less about the loss. Not true. **What hurts more is when people act like your loved one never existed.**

When my friends would come over, I would say: "I know it's awkward for you, so let me just tell you now that we love to talk about Mark." You could see the relief on their faces because they hadn't known what they should do and they hadn't wanted to upset me. Now they knew: It was okay to talk about my husband.

In some cases, your grieving friend may not mind you mentioning their loved one but they may not want to talk about the death itself and what happened — especially if it was an accident, suicide, violent, etc. So be sensitive. And be aware: Some people may not be ready to talk at all. That's why you simply ask. Then you won't have to guess — and/or risk offending or hurting.

Share Stories

One of the things that touched my heart the most was when people would tell me a story about my husband, or talk about how much they missed him or how they cried when they heard the news. These things mean a lot to your grieving friend; it means you cared for their loved one too.

Invite Your Grieving Friend to Share Memories

If you have some quiet time with your grieving friend, ask them to talk about their loved one — what they loved about the person, how the two of them met if the person is their spouse, etc. Ask your friend to tell you stories about their loved one. They may well want to talk. *The night my husband died, two precious friends took me for a walk on the beach with a glass of wine and asked me all about Mark. I loved it! Then they put me in the middle of them in bed and hugged me all night.*

Don't Ask "How Are You Doing?"

Instead of asking your grieving friend how they're doing, ask questions like: "How are you managing?" "How are you coping?" "What are you feeling today?"

People ALWAYS ask each other "how are you?" or "how are you doing?" in everyday life. But they rarely mean it. It's merely a form of greeting in most cases. So questions like "how are you?" will come across to your grieving friend as too casual — like you don't understand the seriousness of what they're going through and you don't really care how they are.

One man in my grief support group said that it bugged him so much when people asked him how he was doing that he once answered: "Like sh__! How do you think I'm doing?" Of course, the person who had asked the question hadn't intended to offend. She was simply trying to reach out. No wonder people are often scared to approach someone who is grieving.

Encourage Your Grieving Friend
to Be Careful About Major Decisions

You always hear that you're not supposed to make any major decisions for a year after a death. It's good advice. Who you are when someone dies is not the same person you will be a year later. You will not be thinking the same way. Sometimes you're not thinking at all in the moment, even though what you're doing seems very logical to you.

It's normal that your grieving friend may just want to escape from it all — sell the house, move away, quit their job — as they want to get away from the pain and the memories. These are decisions they might regret later. So again: **Encourage your friend to be cautious.**

Help Your Grieving Friend Deal with
Clothing and Other Personal Items

I wanted to immediately purge my house of all my husband's personal belongings — clothes, tools, etc. I wanted to keep pictures, but I found Mark's things in my drawers to be such a painful reminder. I realized that, even though I wanted to get rid of the items today, I could feel much differently a few months later. So I decided to pack all of Mark's things up and put them in the garage. Then, in a year or so, I could revisit what I wanted to do with it all; I'd still be left with the choice.

Encourage your grieving friend to use a similar strategy. They don't have to keep clothing and personal items in the house itself. But it might be good to keep them for a while — packed up in boxes in the garage or in a similar outside place.

Getting rid of clothing may seem like something that could be done quickly and early on but keep in mind that it can be used to make memory blankets, to create something else memorable, or they may want to wear some of the loved one's clothes. *I have three favorite shirts of Mark's that I love to wear!*

Use Caution When It Comes to Current Events

Be cautious with talk about current events, or with other normal small talk, especially early on. **It can be hurtful to your grieving friend when they are crushed beyond repair and the people around them act like nothing has changed.** There is a time to distract. But for the first little while in particular, be aware that efforts to distract may do damage instead, if only unintentionally.

AS LIFE GOES ON

Stay in Contact with Your Grieving Friend for the Long Haul

Everyone told me that most people would be gone after the memorial service, and that was pretty accurate. One of the hardest things for me was that many people had promised my son that they would reach out to him and keep in touch, as they knew he would be missing his dad. But none of them did. I think they had good intentions, but you would not believe how painful it is when people don't follow through. They get busy with their own lives and forget.

This may seem like a simple solution, but it really does help: **Make a note on your calendar to call your grieving friend periodically.** *I started doing this for others I wanted to continue reaching out to after their losses. If I wrote on the calendar to call them once a month, I did. If I left it up to me remembering, it probably didn't happen.*

Please don't forget about your grieving friend. They will hurt for a long, long time.

Encourage Your Grieving Friend to Join a Support Group

I joined a grief group within two weeks of my husband's death, as I was desperate for help. I don't think most people would do that on their own. Some people just aren't ready for a group right away. But the grief group was invaluable to me. It was the one place where I felt I could share how I was really feeling and people would understand. I was at times so hopeless and sad, making sobbing sounds I didn't know were possible, that I thought even my friends and family wouldn't really know what to do if they saw me like that. I was not comfortable sharing my pain and confusion with them. But I could with my grief group.

GriefShare is an international organization with groups all over the world. You can find out about it at *GriefShare.org*. Maybe, if your grieving friend doesn't want to go to a meeting by themselves, you could take them the first time. *I loved the content of the sessions, but I found the first group I attended not to be a good fit for me. So I tried another GriefShare group and it was a much better fit. Same content as the first group, but the group matched me better. We were kindred spirits.*

Whether your grieving friend attends GriefShare meetings or not, they can sign up to receive a **daily email from the organization for one year**. *These emails were amazing to me! They usually spoke to me right where I was, and they were a wonderful source of truth, encouragement, and direction the first year after I lost my husband. I couldn't wait to get them every day.*

Help Write a Letter Explaining What's Happened

After the funeral service and when things have calmed down a bit, help your grieving friend write a letter explaining what's happened. Send it to people who don't yet know but would want to — like the people on your grieving friend's Christmas card list. *I wish I had done this. I didn't know how, so I didn't, and many people were shocked a year later when they found out my husband had died. One of my friends sent out a beautiful letter after her son died, explaining to all what had happened. It was a great way to notify people.*

Be a Close Companion

I had a friend who committed to staying with me a couple of days a month for the entire first year after my husband's death. I kept telling her I didn't need her, and I honestly believed that. But every time she came I saw that I really did need her; her presence was such a comfort and help to me.

Consider Giving a Pet

A pet may be a wonderful distraction for your grieving friend — or it may not be. Think hard before you bring your friend a new pet, especially a puppy.

That said: All the people I know who were given a pet after they suffered a loss thought they didn't want it, yet they ended up loving it, as it gave them a companion to love and hold; it filled a need. But this doesn't mean your friend will react the same way, so make sure you have a back-up plan if they don't want the pet or it doesn't work out.

Remember Holidays

Send a card on holidays, the lost loved one's birthday, or the anniversary of the lost loved one's death. If your grieving friend lost a spouse, even a card on their wedding anniversary or on Valentine's Day is touching.

A dear friend brought me a single rose on my wedding anniversary with a little note that said, simply: "Love, Mark." Oh, what that meant to me! For two widows, on

Valentine's Day, I secretly dropped off some special deco-rated chocolates and a single rose, along with a card saying: "Thinking of you today, as I know you will be remember-ing and missing your Valentine." They didn't need to know it was from me. That made it more fun and mysterious!

If your friend lost a parent or child, please remember them on Mother's Day and Father's Day.

Be Understanding About Special Occasions

If you have something like a birthday party or holiday occa-sion, let your grieving friend know that you would love to have them take part — but that you also understand if they're not up to it. Give them the choice.

This can be extremely uncomfortable; sometimes it's awkward to even approach a grieving person about such an event. But you'll be glad you did.

If your grieving friend's loved one would normally have been attending the function with them, you may want to set a place for the missing person at the table, or at least acknowledge the missing person in some way. It's a lovely gesture — acknowledgment of what's been lost. You could tell your friend that you would like to acknowledge the lost loved one and ask how they may want it to be done or if they mind your ideas, like a toast, etc. *My first Thanksgiving after Mark died was really hard. It was our first family gath-ering since his death. I thought those gathered would say something about him or set a place for him, but they didn't say a word. It was like he hadn't existed. I was crushed. But when I talked to my family members about it, I realized that they were not being inconsiderate. They were actually trying to be the opposite. They were afraid that talking about Mark might upset me. It's easy to have miscommunications when we don't talk about these things. I don't think I knew how to approach them or they knew how to approach me.* I believe one of the most helpful ways to deal with the awkwardness that happens at these times is for everyone to gather and one person says, "Let's acknowledge that we are feeling the loss of Mark today. We miss him. He should be here. It hurts. Let's laugh when we want to laugh and cry when we want to cry. Let's talk about him. Let's not pretend." When that is addressed at the beginning, it releases tension and makes everyone feel better, because it is usually the elephant in the room. It is freeing!

Offer to Help Coordinate a "Memory Night"

One of the GriefShare daily emails suggests having a "Memory Night" to help remember the person who died. Here's what it can look like:

- Plan a time to meet together as a group.
- To begin the Memory Night, light a candle to symbolize the one who is not there.
- Have others ask the grieving person random questions about the loved one who has died to get to know the deceased individual better. "What do you miss the

most about your loved one?" "What places or smells bring back special memories?" Let the person talk.

- Let everyone else in attendance share something about the lost loved one too — a memory, what they miss, words they would always say.

- After about an hour of questions, tears, and sharing, take time to respond to the grieving person. **This is not a time for platitudes and advice,** but for a pouring out of love and connectedness from one heart to another.

- You could end here or have a prayer time. Have the grieving person sit in the center of the group, and people who want to can lay their hands on the bereaved person. Or, if the bereaved person is uncomfortable, have everyone stay where they are. There are many ways to do it.

Bill Dunn and Kathy Leonard, *Through a Season of Grief*, Thomas Nelson, 2004, p. 353

Know That Setbacks Are Normal

Don't worry if your grieving friend seems to be making progress and then slips backward. This is a roller coaster ride of a journey, and ups and downs are to be expected. It's all part of the process, and it can last for years.

Two and a half years after Mark's death, I felt like I was doing quite well. But one day, when I was going on a business trip, I was not prepared for what happened when I got near my gate at the local airport. I remembered vividly the times Mark and I were in that airport, and I totally lost it! It was like a huge wave had knocked me down. It came out of nowhere. And these waves of emotion will continue to come.

Know That "Well" Will Take a Long Time

Don't keep wanting to hear that your grieving friend is doing well. They won't be "well" for quite some time.

I found that people wanted to hear I was doing better and that I was okay. But the reality was that sometimes I was doing okay and other times I was in the depths of despair.

There is no timeframe for grief. We expect people to be over their grief so quickly in the Western world. It makes many of us uncomfortable or embarrassed to tell people we are still suffering. *I was in more pain the second year than the first — because by then the shock had worn off and reality had set in.* One of my friends, who had lost her son tragically in an accident, came to comfort me when Mark died. She said that since it had been five years since her son had died, she would never admit to anyone that she was still grieving. She didn't think they would understand.

How sad is that? And you know what? If I hadn't lost my husband, I would have been one of those who hadn't understood.

Just because someone looks good doesn't mean they are good. Be patient and understanding.

Don't Get Distracted

As much as you think you'll be there for your grieving friend in the future, it's so easy to get distracted with life. **As time goes on, it will be difficult to remember to care for your friend. So please plan it.** Did you notice that I've said this before? It bears repeating.

Take a few minutes each week or every other week to give your grieving friend a phone call, write them a note, or drop by their house. You could even write notes, then address and stamp them ahead of time and have them ready to go as needed — which would then require no time at all.

Confession: *You would assume that I would easily reach out to my grieving friends, since I know how deep the pain goes and how much they need our care. It's pretty easy in the beginning. But then, I find it takes more and more effort. It's work. It takes planning, and it takes time away from other things I may want to do. Maybe someone else will take care of my friend, I think to myself. How terrible is that? I'm ashamed to admit this, but I have to share it with you —* **because if helping for the long haul is hard for someone who has already lost a loved one, how much harder is it for someone who hasn't?**

So again, let me remind you that **this does take work, effort, and planning — and you won't always want to do it.** You'll get tired. Especially as time goes by and you move on with your life while your grieving friend is still stuck. **You won't have the same sympathy, understanding, or**

patience as you had before. If your grieving friend is close to you, you may have to give more time, more care, and more of yourself than you ever imagined. But I promise you: Every effort you make will mean so much to them. It shows them that someone cares and that their suffering is not forgotten. **You are desperately needed — and you really do make a difference.**

Please Don't Forget

Name: _____

Children's names: _____

Lost loved one's name:_____

Mark the Following Dates on Your Calendar:

Lost loved one's date of birth: _____

Lost loved one's date of death: _____

Wedding anniversary: _____

Children's birthdays: _____

- Make a note on the calendar if any of these holidays pertain to the grieving person's loss: Valentine's Day, Mother's Day, Father's Day.
- Send special cards on holidays and key dates. Make them or buy them ahead of time so that you're ready.
- Send gifts.
- Attend milestones of children if the lost loved one was a parent.

A Few Things You Can Do to Help Your Grieving Friend:

- Call them.
- Text them and don't be surprised if there is no response, but keep doing it.
- Take them to lunch.
- Take them to a movie.
- Take them for a walk.

- Take them for a weekend away.
- Bring them a favorite meal.
- Help them with house projects.
- Make a time to see them so that you can listen and let them talk.

If Your Grieving Friend Lives Far Away:

- Call them regularly.
- Text them.
- Send cards, especially for the first year after the loss.
- Give them a blanket of comfort.
- Send gift cards.
- Later on, when people have forgotten, send flowers, chocolates, or little gifts just to remind them you care.

Don't Forget the Children!

If you would like to print out a copy of this form, please visit GriefandTraumaHealing.com.

I don't have the words
to make you feel better,
but I do have the arms to give
you a hug, ears to listen to
whatever you want to talk about,
and I have a heart; a heart that
is aching to see you smile again.

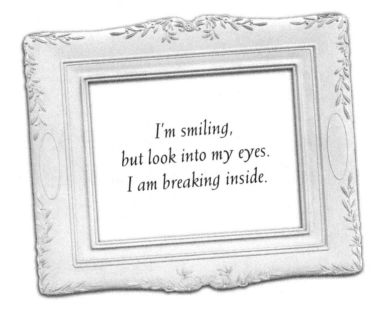

I'm smiling,
but look into my eyes.
I am breaking inside.

Sympathy Cards

WHY IS IT SO HARD TO FIGURE OUT WHAT TO WRITE IN A sympathy card? Here are some examples to get you started.

My thoughts and prayers are with you in this time of great sorrow.

Words cannot express how sorry I am. We all have lost a very dear person. Please know that I'm praying for all of you.

It's with a heavy heart that I send my condolences and my sympathy to [loved one's family names]. [Loved one] was a true and loving friend who made me laugh, and at times made me cry. I will miss her smile, her voice, and her laugh. She has left me with many good memories that I will carry inside my heart forever. May God be with you all during your time of loss.

Know that I will keep you all in my thoughts and, most of all, in my prayers.

May God wrap His loving arms around you and give you peace and comfort. [Loved one] will be missed by so many.

[Loved one] was a good friend of mine. We went to school together. My heart is hurting. I will miss her so much. Love and prayers to her family.

[Loved one] was always such a wonderful lady. What I remember most is her beautiful smile and sweet voice. I'm so sorry for your loss.

Words cannot express the sympathy I feel for [loved one's] wife, children, father, and brothers. I am truly sorry for the loss of such a beautiful person. We had some great memories together, and I'll never forget him.

I was so saddened to hear about [loved one]. [Loved one's family names] ... my thoughts and prayers are with you. I have such good memories of [loved one] from high school. Heaven surely received a sweet soul.

I am so very sorry.

I cannot imagine your pain. My heart is with you.

There is nothing that can take away the pain you feel. I offer my sincere condolences.

The loss of [loved one] has left a void that can never be filled. I am very sorry for your loss.

I am sending you a hug, as there are no words to say.

[Loved one] was a gift to us. He will never be forgotten. Our thoughts and prayers are with you.

I love you, my friend, and would take this pain away if I could.

Please accept our deepest condolences on the loss of [loved one].

Our sincerest sympathy on the tragic passing of [loved one]. He will be missed!

We were shocked to hear of [loved ones's] death. Our thoughts are with you during this difficult time. We are here for you.

Thinking of you and praying for you.

You will never be far from our thoughts and prayers. We are your friends ... and we are not going anywhere. We are here for you in any way you may need us. You are loved!

With deepest sympathy.

Our hearts are very heavy and sad. We miss our friend already. Our condolences.

Wishing you peace to bring comfort, courage to face the days ahead, and loving memories to cherish forever. Please accept our heartfelt sympathies.

We are truly stunned and so sorry to hear about [loved one]. They were one of the kindest, nicest people we have ever met. The world is definitely not a better place now. They will be missed.

Words cannot express the sadness we feel over your loss. We are mourning with you.

I am so sorry for the great, great loss. My thoughts and prayers are with you. I miss him/her too!

By the way: **You might also want to send your grieving friend a card at other key times in the year** or so after their loss — to acknowledge their loved one's birthday, for example, or your friend's birthday, or their anniversary or Valentine's Day, or the anniversary of their loved one's death, or Mother's Day or Father's Day, or Thanksgiving or Christmas or even the long holiday weekends associated with them (I was shocked at how tough those long weekends were for me).

Summary

A FEW HANDY LISTS TO REMIND YOU
HOW TO HELP YOUR GRIEVING FRIEND

Here are some things you can
bring to your grieving friend:

- Meals
- Breakfast foods (bagels, cream cheese, yogurt, casserole)
- Snacks for your friend and their visitors
- Juice
- Soda
- Bottles of water
- Paper plates
- Paper cups
- Plastic utensils

- Paper napkins
- Paper towels
- Tissues

Here are some things you can do for or give to your grieving friend:

- Start a notebook for them to keep track of everything.
- Start a memory page for the lost loved one on Facebook or somewhere else.
- Make calls.
- Watch the children.
- Walk the dog.
- Take the dog to the groomers.
- Clean the cat litter.
- Do the laundry.
- Mop the floor.
- Take the trash out.
- Strip and make the beds.
- Clean the house.
- Wash the dishes.
- Help with household repairs.
- Run errands.
- Take your friend for a walk.
- Hire a cleaning service for the day and take your friend out.

When your grieving friend is a man:

- Just talk to him and ask how he's managing. Most people miss the talking if their loved one lived with them. Try to fill this emptiness at times by coming over or taking your friend out, or even calling and simply LETTING him talk. *I used to tell my husband everything about my day. Now, no one wants to hear it.*

- If he doesn't know how to cook, teach him how to make a few basic or favorite meals — or, better yet, bring them to him.

- Show him the ropes of taking care of a house if he's not used to it — how and when to water the plants, do the laundry, perform simple housecleaning.

- Serve as his housekeeper for a day.

- Give him a massage gift certificate.

- Give him a memory keychain.

- Give him a blanket of comfort. (See page 48.)

- If he lost a spouse, send flowers on his anniversary.

- If he lost a child, acknowledge it on the child's birthday or Father's Day.

- Take him out for his favorite hobby or sport.

- Take him to a movie and dinner.

- Watch the children so he can get away or take a nap.

- Send him a Basket of Blessings — a basket full of goodies he would like: favorite treats or foods, DVDs or CDs, a favorite magazine, or perhaps tickets to a ball game.

When your grieving friend is a woman:

- Schedule a couple of men to come to her house and do handyman work (especially if she lost her husband).
- Give her a massage gift certificate. *One of my friends called me up saying she had two certificates for an afternoon spa treatment and wondered if I would go with her. I immediately said yes, as it sounded nice and she wasn't going to have to pay for me since she already had the certificates. It was a wonderfully refreshing time. When we were leaving, I saw my friend go to the counter and pay the lady! What? "I thought you had gift certificates," I said. "Yes, I know," she replied. "You wouldn't have come with me unless I told you that." My friend had a big smile on her face. She was sneaky and sweet. And she was right.* You might consider using this type of approach yourself — especially if you have a friend who finds it difficult to accept help from people or who feels she is putting someone out.
- Give her a manicure or pedicure.
- Send her a Basket of Blessings — a basket full of goodies she would like: lavender or calming lotion, candles, oils, chocolate, cookies, gift cards, DVDs or CDs, a favorite magazine, perhaps tickets to a play or concert.

- Send flowers on her anniversary if she lost her spouse.
- Give her a memory necklace.
- Give her a blanket of comfort. (See page 48.)
- Serve as housekeeper for a day.
- Take her to a movie and dinner.
- Pick her up and take her to a quiet place for lunch; let her talk about where she is in her grief journey.
- Watch the children so she can get away or take a nap.
- If she lost a child, acknowledge it on the child's birthday or Mother's Day.
- If she is a widow, she may suffer financially if her husband was the major supporter. Help her with — or get someone to figure out — her financial situation and plan accordingly. This can be completely overwhelming, especially if the husband took care of all the finances. There is a great book for this task called *Moving Forward on Your Own: A Financial Guidebook for Widows*, by Kathleen M. Rehl. It would be a very useful gift for your friend.

When your grieving friend is a child:

- Talk to them about their lost loved one.
- Give them big hugs.
- Give them coupons for movies, ice cream, coffee, etc.
- Take them out for a fun event.

- Give them a special stuffed animal.
- Give them a blanket of comfort. (See page 48.)
- Write to them to remind them that you're thinking about them.
- If a special milestone, like a graduation, comes up, consider attending it and acknowledging that the lost loved one is missing and that it must be hard, but that you think the child is special and you want to share this day with them.
- A simple book written to show children and adults that they are never alone is *The Invisible String*, by Patrice Karst.

Some gifts/gestures that are appropriate for anyone who has lost someone:

- The book *Tear Soup: A Recipe for Healing After Loss*, by Pat Schwiebert and Chuck DeKlyen. It's a beautifully illustrated, short guide that affirms the bereaved in a simple way. It would be appropriate for adults or children.
- Gift cards.
- A Basket of Blessings — a basket filled with treats, fun things … anything that might be helpful.
- A memory necklace.
- A memory keychain.
- A memory stone.
- A blanket of comfort. (See page 48.)

- A pet.
- A memory book made up of a page from different friends or family members who each provide a favorite picture of the lost loved one, along with a story about the person or what they loved or miss most about the person.
- A tribute book with any correspondence the grieving person might want to save about their lost loved one, before or after the death — emails, cards, notes, etc. Add pictures, even from the funeral or memorial service, or do whatever you want. You could collect all the material from your grieving friend and put it together.
- Frame a picture of the lost loved one.
- Make a booklet of all the memories or comments posted on the Facebook memory page.
- Jewelry featuring the lost loved one's fingerprint. *I had a beautiful heart pendant, with Mark's fingerprint that was taken at the mortuary, and I wear it as a necklace. I gave my son a keychain with the fingerprint. We both love them! I feel like I am holding Mark's hand when I touch it.*

THE BLANKET OF COMFORT

The Blanket of Comfort that showed up for me in a box one day has been the **best gift I could have ever received** — and I didn't even know I needed it. It's a special blanket made with love and given to me by a friend who wanted me to feel cared for. I wrap this blanket around me when I need a hug. I cling to it when I need a special touch or when I'm crying on the floor. I sleep with it every night. It isn't just any old blanket; it's special. It provides the same feeling that our special blankets did when we were children — the feeling of security.

After experiencing what the comfort blanket did for me, I have since given comfort blankets to others I know who are grieving (as well as to those who are sick or hurting). These blankets can provide comfort in all sorts of situations. When you look at your Blanket of Comfort, you know someone cares for you. The response I get from people who have received these simple blankets melts my heart. Grown ups tell me stories how they use them all the time — even at work, or how they will cherish them the rest of their lives and how it means the world to them. It is a gift of love!

You can make a Blanket of Comfort for your friend. Go to my website *GriefandTraumaHealing.com* for instructions.

Christmas

WHEN THE CHRISTMAS HOLIDAYS COME UP, MAKE SURE YOUR grieving friend is taken care of. They may be too depressed to put up decorations, so tell them you're coming for a day to put the decorations up — and that you will return after the holiday is over to pack the decorations away.

Does your grieving friend have people to spend the holidays with? If the loss is especially fresh, they really might prefer to not be with anyone on Christmas, and that can be okay. Talk to them about it. Give them until the last minute to decide and tell them they can come for as little or as long as they want.

If they decide not to attend, maybe you can ask them if you can come over for a few minutes at the beginning of the day to have a quiet time of coffee or bring a special treat — just to say hello on that holiday, as you know they are not up to a big event or lots of people, but you want to remember them.

Please remember to acknowledge your grieving friend's lost loved one at Christmas. FamilyLife offers a list of great ideas (which I share here with the organization's kind permission).

10 Christmas Gifts or Remembrances for the Brokenhearted

1. A tree that can be planted in the family's yard in memory of the loved one (or a gift certificate to a nursery that can be used to purchase a tree in the spring).

2. Memorials to the local church or charities.

3. A scrapbook filled with pictures of the loved one.

4. Gift certificates to a cabin or lodge, or to a place that the loved one once enjoyed.

5. An original poem about the deceased.

6. A journal from friends and family with written memories about the deceased.

7. Addressing the grieving person's Christmas cards or notes.

8. Joining the grieving person in holiday shopping, or doing the shopping for them.

9. Picking the grieving person up for Christmas services at church and holiday get-togethers.

10. Helping the grieving person shop for that "perfect gift" that they can give to others in memory of their lost loved one.

How to Handle Christmas Cards

Be cautious about sending your grieving friend a typical Christmas card featuring the happy family picture and the letter with all the great things going on in your life. Remember: Your grieving friend's world has come to a sudden halt, and Christmas cards and letters can be a reminder that everyone else's lives have gone on. Some people may find these communications uplifting, but others will find it **extremely painful to see a smiling family or read a Christmas letter** about all the wonderful things that happened to them this year. It highlights what they are missing.

If you do write a Christmas letter you may want to acknowledge hurting friends or family members, by adding a paragraph that addresses them. For example, at the end of her Christmas letter my friend wrote: "We know that the Christmas season is not a happy time for everyone. Unfortunately, some of you are missing loved ones who have passed, or are feeling lonely, depressed or struggling for many reasons. We want you to know that you are not forgotten by us. We are thinking of you and praying for you."

Please consider sending your grieving friend a special Christmas sympathy card. Or send your regular Christmas card but include a special note about your grieving friend's loved one or loss. Here are some suggestions about what you could say:

When someone so loved is gone from the circle, a time like this can tug at the heart.

Quietly, gently may the spirit of the season shine through your shadows and touch your world with warmth and light.

After the loss of a loved one, the holiday season brings special memories of Christmases past and tender moments of sadness.

May God bless you with His love and peace during this holiday season and throughout the coming year.

At this holiday season, we remember and honor those who are no longer with us and cherish those who are.

Wishing you a gentle season of healing and peace.

Wishing you the gift of faith, the blessing of hope, and the peace of His love at Christmas and always.

Thoughts of you fill our minds and hearts during this difficult season. Please know that we care.

During this difficult time, it is hard to celebrate the season with the same joy that everyone else seems to possess. You are loved and cared for, by many. We have not forgotten.

Thinking about you, as we know you are missing your dear son/husband/wife this season. As the world around you seems to go on, we know yours has abruptly stopped. You are deeply loved and deeply cared for and we have not forgotten.

For some more helpful general tips as well as tips for specific types of losses, please see the Appendix.

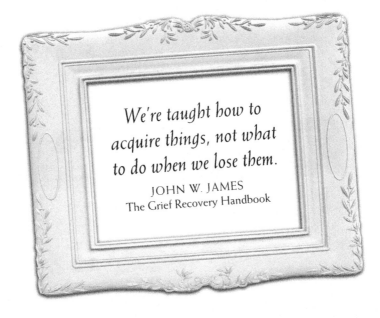

We're taught how to
acquire things, not what
to do when we lose them.

JOHN W. JAMES
The Grief Recovery Handbook

Healing from Loss:
A Proven Method
of Grief Recovery

THE QUESTIONS I GET ASKED MOST OFTEN FROM SOMEONE who is grieving are "How long will this last?" and "Will I ever be happy again?" There is no easy answer.

But I can answer the questions "**Can** my broken heart ever heal?" "**Can** I be happy again?" And the answer is "Yes!" I know it is possible because I experienced healing and have seen countless others experience it as well.

At the beginning of my grief journey, I joined a grief support group, as I mentioned earlier in the book. It was a perfect place for me at that time. I was with others who felt the same way I did. The information and fellowship I received there were helpful, encouraging and invaluable. I would highly recommend these type of support groups. But, it didn't help heal my broken heart and take away the pain, and neither did three years of counseling. Although it was good to have someone to talk to, I had no idea what to do with the pain, and I was stuck in my grief.

Then I experienced the Grief Recovery Method®, which took me through a series of specific action steps to walk through the process of healing from loss. And it worked! I was transformed! It got to the root of my pain and showed me how to release it. **It left me with all the happy memories of my husband without the pain that used to go along with them.** I wanted to live again! A massive heaviness was lifted from me. It led me to discover things I was holding onto and suffering from — things of which I was completely unaware. And it showed me how to let them go and be free!

I now use this method as I work with individuals and groups on Living After Loss and I see the same results. People are being set free from the physical and emotional pain that is caused by unresolved grief.

Let me answer four important questions:

WHAT IS GRIEF?

Grief is the normal and natural reaction to a loss. The range of normal emotions attached to grief is dictated by a person's unique personality and how they express their feelings. A person's grief is about the one-of-a-kind relationship they had with the person who died. No other person had the same relationship. No one knows exactly how that person feels.

6 Myths of Grief

Don't Feel Bad

Replace the Loss

Grieve Alone

Grief Just Takes Time

Be Strong / Be Strong For Others

Keep Busy

Grief Recovery Method®

MYTHS OF GRIEF

The Grief Recovery Method and the Grief Recovery Institute have led the way in educating people about the myths and misinformation surrounding grief. The descriptions below come from them; I have merely added a few of my own thoughts.

Time Heals All Wounds

This concept is probably responsible for more heartache than any other single wrong idea in our society. It isn't true. So many are believing that if they just give it time, they will feel better again. Time itself does not heal; it is what you do within that time that will help you heal. I love the analogy in the Grief Recovery Handbook about discovering your car has a flat tire and just pulling off to the side of the road and waiting for the air to somehow get back in the tire. People are hurting needlessly for years after a loss because they think time will make it better. You must take action to fix the tire. You must take action to heal your broken heart.

Don't Feel Bad

This suggests that feeling bad or sad is not an appropriate reaction to a heart-breaking loss. It is baffling to be told not to feel bad as you try to make sense of the normal and natural emotions you experience, for example when someone meaningful in your life dies.

As human beings, we are equipped with the capacity to feel and express all emotions — happy and sad, and everything in between. But early in life, we are taught to repress or bury our naturally occurring sad or painful feelings. As a child, we are told, "Don't cry," or "Don't cry. Have a cookie. You'll feel better." As we get older, we are expected to "hold it in" and "keep it together." We need the freedom to express all feelings — not just the good ones.

Grieve Alone

Grieving people tend to isolate. We have been taught that we are not to burden others with our feelings. People don't want to see us hurting and, often, don't know what to do with us, so we keep it to ourselves at a time when it is usually much better for us to be with others and participating in activities.

Be Strong

As grievers, we hear that all the time, "You are so strong," "Be strong," or "You must be strong for the children." In attempting to "be strong" or "be strong for others," most people hide their own feelings — at least those that might be visible, such as tears and other natural verbal and non-verbal displays of emotion. In effect, when we "act" strong and cover up our honest emotions, we are lying to those we interact with — not to mention that we may be lying to ourselves.

Replace the Loss

A child loses a pet and what are they told? "Don't feel bad. We will get you another dog." You suffer a relationship break-up and are told "Don't feel bad. There are plenty of fish in the sea." All relationships are unique. There are no exceptions. You cannot replace a relationship. You must grieve and complete your relationships to the person who died, or to the marriage, or romance that ended. Until and unless you do that, you're doomed to drag the past into your present and thereby sabotage your future.

Keep Busy

People would always tell me how good it was for me to "keep busy." And it does temporarily distract you from feeling the pain. But, if we think we're not supposed to feel bad — even though feeling bad or sad is the normal reaction to the loss of any kind — then keeping busy is another way of trying to bypass the normal feelings of sadness and pain associated with loss. We must experience these feelings to heal. Avoiding them is a short-term solution.

All of these myths and misinformation hinder the ability to experience healing.

WHAT IS RECOVERY?

Recovery from loss is the result of a series of steps and choices taken by the one grieving to heal their broken heart. It involves completing all the unfinished business in the relationship that was lost — addressing unmet dreams, hopes and expectations and acknowledging what they wish had been different, better or more. The steps are outlined in the Grief Recovery Method® and done in a safe and supportive environment with a Certified Grief Recovery Specialist®. The grieving person is in control of their recovery, and the specialist is the guide and encourager. Grieving people rarely lack willingness or courage. What they are missing is correct information, the right tools and a safe place to apply them. **The goal is to keep the happy memories, but not the pain.**

WHAT DOES RECOVERY LOOK LIKE?

♡ Feeling better

♡ Recapturing a joy for living

♡ Fond memories can return without the pain (**It doesn't mean you won't be sad at times, as the person is always missed, but the heart-wrenching pain is no longer there.**)

♡ Fully engaging in relationships again

♡ Feelings of freedom and safety

My website has information on working with me in person or online (for people out of the area) on Living After Loss using the Grief Recovery Method®. *www.griefandtrauma-healing.com* You can also look for a Grief Recovery Method group or certified consultant in your area.

If you care for someone who is grieving, a great gift to give is to share the Grief Recovery Method® information with them or consider giving them a gift certificate to attend group or private sessions.

Free downloadable books on various grief topics are available on my website.

It is a great joy in my life to guide hurting people through this life-changing journey.

Do I choose to wake up
every day and grieve?
No, I wake up every day
and know that
part of me is missing.

RENEE SCRIMA

Appendix

DEALING WITH DIFFERENT TYPES OF LOSSES

THERE ARE MANY DIFFERENT TYPES OF LOSSES, AND IT'S impossible to cover them all in this guide. But the following are among the most common.

Here are some tips for helping your grieving friend deal with the aspects that are unique to their specific type of loss.

GENERAL TIPS

- People can expect the grieving person to "move on" or "be over it" quickly. *In my own case, I received many discreet comments about how I should be doing so much better after the first year. I felt guilty that I wasn't. In fact, the second year was even more painful than the first because by then reality had really sunk in. I felt like there was something wrong with me.* **I didn't need guilt on top of grief.**

- LISTEN to the person who is grieving. Don't talk, except to help them continue to share. **Wait for them to ask questions BEFORE you share your own experience.**

- **Don't make the mistake of thinking you KNOW how a person must be feeling. We can't possibly know,** even if we've gone through something similar. My friend said that the people she found most comforting were the ones who seemed to recognize their ignorance, and who saw it as their job to simply listen carefully or just be there with a hug and their presence, making themselves available to ease my friend's struggles in whatever way she communicated.

- It can sure be nice to come home and open your door to flowers or find food on the doorstep. It's just comforting to know that someone is thinking about you. So drop off a little something for your grieving friend, along with a note. It's an especially nice gesture after some time has passed after the loved one's death, and your grieving friend starts to think that no one remembers they're hurting.

- Texts and phone calls can be comforting, but don't be surprised if your grieving friend doesn't respond. Keep sending texts, and keep calling and leaving messages of comfort.

- You can acknowledge the inevitable elephant in the room by simply saying: "I heard about your loss, and I'm so sorry." The more outward everyone is about the loss, the better. **Pretending nothing has happened makes**

the situation seem like it's not a big deal. Yet your grieving friend's pain is still there.

- Asking your grieving friend "what can I do?" is pointless. Just show up! You don't have to offer up amazing advice or incredible insight. Just sit with your friend and listen. Whether it is two minutes or two hours, your presence means you're there for your friend. And that means more than anything.

- Be open and unafraid to speak about the loss.

- Interestingly, many of the people who offered contributions to this book experienced the same thing I did: The SECOND year after the loss is much WORSE than the first. I asked my widowed friend what she was feeling a few days before the first anniversary of her husband's death. Her reply, in a text: "Tearful, sad, blech, lonely."

- Toasting or setting a place for a missing loved one on holidays or for gatherings can be a beautiful way of acknowledging your grieving friend's loss. You may want to ask them about it as not everyone would want this.

- Think long term, not short term. Your grieving friend will need care for some time. They may seem okay or even tell you they're okay — but they aren't.

- Ask your grieving friend to talk about their loved one. My friend, who lost her son, told me it made her day when someone said to her, "Tell me stories about Zach!" If you want to make me light up just say, "Tell me about your husband." Most of us love to talk about our loved ones.

- Family get-togethers can be hard or helpful; it depends on the person. My friend now wishes that she hadn't put herself through them for the first year after her son's death. How could his cousins be having a good time? Of course they should, but their happy sounds hurt my friend's ears and soul. She thought she needed to show the kids that her grief wouldn't interrupt normal celebrations like Christmas and birthdays. But now she wishes she had given herself permission to "take a year off." Those get-togethers were really hard. I don't believe that this is the case for all people who are grieving; I'm sure that some take comfort in being at family celebrations. But you may want to ask your grieving friend what they want to do and give them permission to skip the gatherings for a while or whenever they don't feel up to it. *I felt the same way my friend did; the family gatherings were very hard for me. Even one, two years after my loss, it was difficult. My husband's entire family was there, but his absence was so apparent to me. He should have been there too! I knew it was going to be tough, but I thought I could hold it together for a couple of hours. Sure enough, after two hours, I just broke down and ended up bawling my eyes out. The poor people who had to watch that; you can be sure they weren't expecting it. I left without saying goodbye, and I cried all the way home.*

- Often, the surviving children can be forgotten as people focus on the adults. These children not only have their own suffering over the loss, they're also struggling to understand what's going on with their parent or parents since their grief has changed them. They may worry about them as well. Reach out to these children. Talk to them about what's going on. Take special care of them.

- A good response when someone says how much it hurts: "It should hurt. You loved them, and it is okay to hurt."

- Don't speak "Christian-ese" to your grieving friend. People mean for these types of words to be comforting, and I would have said them myself before my own loss. But they're usually NOT very helpful during the initial pain of loss.

- Don't try to make your grieving friend feel better. Just hug them, hold them, let them cry, or speak their loved one's name. **You can't take away the pain. You don't need to — and you're not required to.**

- Let your grieving friend express their feelings and figure out grief in their own way, with no limits on time. **Be there without platitudes. Your presence alone can be a present.**

LOSS OF A SPOUSE

- When your friend loses a spouse, understand that all areas of their life are impacted. *When I lost my husband, I lost my dreams for the future with him. I lost my best friend, my lover, the father of my child, my financial provider, my chef, my barbecue guy, my comforter, my protector, the only person who would let me tell him about my day and actually care, my TV and movie watching buddy, my handyman, my computer repair guy, my electronics whiz, the grandfather to my future grandchildren.* A widower might lose his lover, his best friend, his cheerleader, his clothing stylist, his housekeeper, his grocery shopper, his cook, his child caretaker, his tutor, his chauffeur, his bookkeeper, his decorator, his gardener, the person who takes care of all the household business and phone calls that need to be made, etc. Do you see the impact? Your grieving friend has lost SO MUCH!

- Your grieving friend might not know anything about the finances or car repairs or cooking meals or taking care of the plants. Come over and teach your friend those things.

- Your grieving friend may feel awkward being around couples, since your friend used to be part of a couple too.

- People tend to focus on the grieving spouse but can easily disregard the loss to the children — who need just as much care and attention.

LOSS OF A SIBLING

- The loss of a sibling is probably the most overlooked or forgotten type of loss. People don't pay much attention to it, yet it's as traumatic as the other types of loss. If your friend has lost a sibling, they have lost someone who was a part of them, who they grew up with and have a long history with. They have lost the aunt or uncle of their children, and another child of their parents. No one knows them like their sibling did. Family gatherings will never be the same.

MISCARRIAGE/STILLBIRTH

- Miscarriages and stillborn births are devastating and, unfortunately, very common. People just don't talk about them very much. One woman told me that the best thing someone said to her after her miscarriage was: "I'm so sorry you have to go through this. Miscarriages suck!" There was something so real and honest and simple in this comment. It validated her feelings.

- The mother can feel guilty in a miscarriage/stillbirth situation: "Was it my fault?" "Could I have done something to prevent it?" "Does my husband blame me?" The mother can feel responsible since her body was carrying the baby. She can be ashamed and feel like she failed. So she needs reassurance, especially from her spouse and/or family.

- Please, please don't say: "At least you have other children."

- Remember that your grieving friend is mourning not just the lost child, but the loss of all the dreams that come with having a child. Your friend is left with empty dreams — and an empty belly that was once filled with life.

- A stillborn should be treated like any unexpected loss of a child. The worst thing you can do is NOT acknowledge your grieving friend's loss.

- Remember that the father in a miscarriage/stillborn situation suffers a loss as well and has incredible heartbreak.

- When a woman becomes pregnant after a miscarriage or stillbirth, don't be surprised if her excitement is tempered by nervousness and anxiety due to the reality of what could come — a reality she has already experienced firsthand.

LOSS OF A CHILD (YOUNG OR ADULT)

- The loss of a child is the most devastating experience a parent can face. Your grieving friend's life will never be the same.

- The loss of a child can take a toll on a marriage, as the parents often grieve differently or blame each other. They can become isolated or experience guilt as well.

- If your grieving friend has other children, your friend needs to continue caring for them and helping them deal with the pain THEY are experiencing because of the loss. So help your friend with their household and child responsibilities as often as you can. Anything you do will be appreciated. Bring your friend a special meal. Invite them out. Watch the children so that they and their spouse can have a weekend alone or away.

- Your grieving friend may fear losing other children or loved ones.

- Keep the lost child's memory alive by using his/her name and talking about him/her when you're with your grieving friend.

MIDLIFE LOSS OF PARENTS

- It's common for an adult who has lost a parent to feel guilty: "I should have taken the keys away sooner." "I should have gone to the doctor with him." "I should have moved closer so I could go over and help more." "Could I have prevented this?" "I resented having to take care of her, and now she's gone." Your grieving friend may not want to express these types of feelings to anyone, but please be aware that your friend is probably experiencing some of them. A good comment might be: **"Losing your parents must be changing your life and how you thought your next few years would be."** This gives your friend the opportunity to talk about their loss IF they want to.

- **The longer in life we have our parents, the more they've been part of — or at least witness to — the many stages:** our childhood, our teenage years, our college years, our wedding, our kids, our career mistakes, our start-overs.

Nothing has ever happened without them knowing, having an opinion, celebrating, disapproving, helping, quietly leaving us be, or somehow reacting. We are fortunate because many people are denied this relationship. However, our identity is fashioned around this primary relationship with our parents. **They are in our heads as well as our hearts.** If we are not identifying with them, we are reacting against them. But one way or another, our parents are the pivot around which we revolve, whether we want it that way or not. So when we lose them, we can be totally adrift, without a mooring. **Often this is surprising.** We can live far away from our parents and feel quite independent. We think we will miss them when they're gone, **but we often aren't prepared for the empty spot in our soul,** and our sense of the disarray of our own being, when we realize how few people are left who REALLY know us like our parents do. One of my friends lost her mother ten years ago. She's still hurting; she still misses her mom so much.

- If your grieving friend cared for their lost parent, they might lose their identity now that the parent has died — as their life was centered on taking care of the parent. Now what will they do?

- There is also a rearranging of one's position in the hierarchy of the family. **There is no longer a protection against the fears of the unknown, no longer a comfortable distance between oneself and death. Our parents are**

always one step closer to these realities, and thus, they serve as a sort of buffer against them. When my friend lost her parent, some people actually said to her: "You're next up!" It was true, and she did feel that way, but she didn't need to hear that. She found the experience very disconcerting and unreal, like she had fallen into an alternate universe.

- Your grieving friend might now be responsible for all the legal and bureaucratic details of their parent's death. It can be a part- or even full-time job to sort it all out, and it takes a lot of energy and organizing. So it might be nice for you to come over and do the vacuuming while your friend is working on the paperwork or organizing the estate papers. Afterwards the two of you can go to lunch and/or a movie.

- When it's time to clear out and dispose of belongings in the family home, ask your grieving friend how you can help. This task is fraught with emotional minefields, not to mention a tremendous amount of confusing decision making that your friend likely hasn't encountered before.

LOSS BY SUICIDE

- There are some very powerful feelings that can go along with a loss due to suicide: guilt, rage, anger, shame. They can attack full force and break your grieving friend's soul.

- Your friend might be angry that the loss has changed their life forever; angry that they were the one who found the person who took their own life and that now they have to live with that vision and trauma; angry that, if they lost their spouse, they are now left to help their children pick up the pieces.

- Suicide has such a stigma attached to it that your friend may also be feeling shame, as if they are being judged because the person who died by suicide. A woman told me she felt like she was marked with a scarlet letter because her husband had killed himself. So remind your friend that you still feel the same about them.

- People who have lost someone to suicide might ask: "Why? Why?" "What did I miss?" "What could I have done to prevent this?" "Why wasn't I there to help?" "Why didn't I protect him/her?"

- Your grieving friend may experience additional physical and emotional trauma if they discovered the person who took their own life.

- Don't mention how the person died. When you're telling someone about it or talking about it, especially in front of your grieving friend, note that your friend lost their loved one a year ago — not that the loved one committed suicide a year ago. This is not the remembrance or legacy of your friend's loved one that your friend wants to hear.

- Don't judge the person who died. They were in extreme pain that we can't imagine. They had lost hope. They may have been struggling with a mental illness and concluded that they just didn't belong. We don't know, and we have no right to judge.

- My friend told me that when she mentioned her brother's suicide to his former high school principal, the principal's words were a great comfort: "Sometimes people who are so extraordinary, such as William, feel as if they don't belong here on Earth with us. They have bigger and better things to do and need to go home sooner than we want them to." This may not be an appropriate thing to say to everyone, but it helped her.

LOSS BY MURDER

- This is an extraordinary event. Your grieving friend was not expecting it at all, so they are going through shock and trauma. Some people in this situation can suffer from Post-Traumatic Stress Disorder (PTSD).

- Your grieving friend may not want to talk about how their loved one died. So don't ask about the details unless your friend wants to share them.

- When talking about the loss with someone, especially your grieving friend, **don't refer to the way the person died**: "She lost her beloved daughter last year"— not "Her beloved daughter was murdered last year."

- Understandably, your grieving friend is probably angry at the person who took their loved one's life.

- Your friend may receive media attention and be involved with the police and the courts. So make sure someone is protecting your friend and helping them deal with it all — or being their representative.

- Your grieving friend may suffer from anxiety and fear, as the world does not seem safe anymore. They may also worry about the loved ones they have left.

Helping Children
Deal with Loss

Listen with your heart, not your head.

Allow all emotions to be expressed, without judgement, criticism, or analysis.

Recognize that grief is emotional, not intellectual.

Avoid the trap of asking your child what is wrong, for he or she will automatically say, "Nothing."

Adults — Go first.

Telling the truth about your own grief will make your child feel safe in opening up about his or her own feelings.

Remember that each of your children is unique.

Each child has a unique relationship to the loss event.

Be patient.

Don't force your child to talk.

Never say "Don't feel sad" or "Don't feel scared."

Sadness and fear, the two most common feelings attached to loss of any kind, are essential to being human.

When Their World Stops
CHEAT SHEET

Don't Say This...	Instead Say...
	I am free on Saturday. I am coming over to help with whatever you need. Make a list.
Let me know if there's anything I can do.	
Stop hanging on and move past it.	When do you feel the closest to him?
Just have faith that this happened for a reason.	You don't deserve this. I'm so sorry.
At least you've still got _____.	What about her are you missing the most today?
Be thankful you had him at all.	I miss him too and I am thankful for you.

When it hurts to look back,
and you're afraid to look
ahead; look beside you and
there will be your friends.

AUTHOR UNKNOWN

About the Author

ANNE-MARIE LOCKMYER IS AN AWARD-WINNING AUTHOR AND speaker, Advanced Grief Recovery Specialist®, and Founder of the Grief and Trauma Healing Network. As a sudden widow herself, Anne-Marie is passionate about helping people in two areas:

1. guiding them through the journey of healing from the pain of grief, loss or trauma — to experience freedom and rediscover joy.
2. equipping them to support loved ones who are suffering from grief.

Anne-Marie works with individuals, groups, and businesses in person and online. If you are interested in working with Anne-Marie, contact her on her website:

GriefandTraumaHealing.com
or
help@griefandtraumahealing.com

*The resources available to help people
who are grieving are continually changing.
For a current list of books, organizations, and resources,
to help someone you know who is grieving,
please check out my website at:
GriefandTraumaHealing.com.*

If you enjoyed this book, please consider
taking a few moments to write a short review of it.
Thank you!

Made in the USA
Monee, IL
20 March 2024